# *the* DIGNITY *of* WORK IN NEW YORK

Tanya W. Ross

Book design by The Troy Book Makers
Printed in the United States of America
The Troy Book Makers • Schodack Landing, New York • thetroybookmakers.com

To order additional copies of this title,
contact your favorite local bookstore
or visit www.shoptbmbooks.com

ISBN: 979-8-90098-046-1

# Contents

# INTRODUCTION

This book shines a light on the often-unrecognized heroes—the men and women whose labor powers New York State, day in and day out. In a state where nearly 80 percent of businesses are classified as small, it's these workers who form the beating heart of New York's essential workforce, quietly sustaining the state's dynamic production.

While policymakers and officials might set broad priorities, the real guardians of safety and health in the workplace are the competent persons, safety and health inspectors, and workers on the site. These individuals shoulder the daily responsibility of making sure that work environments are safe and healthy—a task that is both demanding and all too often taken for granted.

Drawing on decades of firsthand experience as an industrial hygienist, the author brings a unique and credible perspective to these tasks. For twenty years, visits to hundreds of high-risk, small businesses across upstate New York revealed a world where companies rely on whatever tools and machinery they can acquire or maintain on site. Sometimes this equipment is over a century old, a testament to both its utility and the ingenuity of workplaces who keep the equipment running.

The photographs gathered here strive to honor the labor and lives of everyday workers in fields such as construction, manufacturing, healthcare, and equipment maintenance. Through their skill, dedication, and quiet artistry, these workers embody the spirit and dignity needed by so many industries. Their stories are woven deeply into the fabric of our society. Without them, the lifestyle and ease we enjoy today would simply not be possible.

This book invites you to witness and appreciate the essential workers whose dignity and perseverance keep our society thriving. The author hopes the readers will be energized by the workers shown in this book. Both union workers and non-union workers are captured in these pages. This book should educate, inspire, and capture your attention, as much as provide enjoyment.

# Chapter One

# CONSTRUCTION

Rehabilitation of a church window by removing caulking material.

Drilling composite block. Water is used at the drill point to reduce the dust.

Cutting large composite blocks into pieces.
Again, water is used at the saw point to cut down on the silica dust.

An Italian Sculptor hired by the church,
is proud of his architectural ornamentation.

The author is setting up an air pump to collect and
evaluate the environment for air particulates & contaminants.

Working in high places to paint the underside of the building.

Workers are drilling under a road to install a sewer pipe. The terrain is difficult, so the workers, pipe, and drill, are protected by a trench box.

In road construction, grinding and milling paving from the
road surface and loading the asphalt tailings in a truck for transport.

Then, measuring the depth of the milled surface to prepare for the new paving.

At another site, grinding off the concrete on a Canal Lock
to prepare the surface for new reinforced concrete.

Resurfacing the concrete walls of a Canal Lock with rebar reinforcements.

And working on concrete resurfacing in a Canal Lock sluiceway.

This picture shows painting a waste treatment
tank while the worker is lying on his back.

Also shown, a painter is standing on a scaffold to paint the top part.
The area is all enclosed and unventilated so workers wear PPE
(personal protective equipment) to protect against fumes.

An air powered jackhammer is used to bust up the decking on a bridge, while avoiding dust and noise hazards by again using PPE.

Next, workers are preparing the bridge substructure for new decking.

A construction worker is cutting concrete block while
protected against dust and noise hazards, but lacks the
needed ventilation. Note the strength his arms use.

Lumberjacks also wear PPE while felling trees.

Shown here workers are moving a large piece of equipment that is air-lifted by a crane seven stories high. The window was removed to bring it in using a hand truck.

# Chapter Two

# Metal Working

A welder clamps two metal pieces together so they can be fused.

In other metal fabrication, metalsmiths are used to fabricate jewelry.

A bench jeweler inserts gems into a jewelry piece.

This worker is assembling a salt spreader tank.

A Metal Lathe Operator shapes materials by rotating a workpiece while a cutting tool is applied. This is used to create symmetrical and cylindrical shapes.

A punch press operator works with a piercing tool
to make precision holes in metal objects.

The supervisor says, "You see this? This is what we need to do."

Workers are manufacturing and assembling aluminum ladders.

The worker is operating a drill press machine that works on aluminum metal.

At a boiler manufacturer, boiler makers assemble a large tank.

Manufacturing steel wire, and testing it for quality control.
The wire is wound into spools for further use.

[ABOVE] Here, a welder is manufacturing the supporting steel struts for a horse trailer.

[AT RIGHT] To make a product smoother, a worker grinds the metal edges.

Also part of metal working, an electrician assembles an apparatus.

[ABOVE] Manufacturing bicycles involves workers assembling frames, wheels, spokes, pedals, etc.

[AT RIGHT] This worker is spray painting a bicycle frame.

Foundry workers clean up recently cast parts by
blasting sand to polish and get rid of rough edges.

# Chapter Three

# Material Production

[AT RIGHT] This shows measuring the components for creating artistic encaustic paints (a special combination of pigments and hot wax).

[BELOW] The worker is milling the pigment to make the particles so fine they appear to dissolve.

The worker is spooling thread (guiding the thread onto spools) which will be used to make fabric.

These spools will then provide thread to the loom which will make the fabric.

Hot Tub fabrication and manufacturing occurs here.
Plastic sheets are heated and then vacuum formed to a mold of
finished specifications. The worker is needed to operate the process.

This cabinet maker is working on a piece of plastic
material which will be assembled into a cabinet later.

Slate is mined from the ground. Large chunks
of slate are cut into slabs for further processing.

The worker in the back is overseeing an enclosed saw which turns large slate pieces into slate blocks. The closer worker is splitting the block to make slate tiles.

Finally, the slate tiles are trimmed by circular blades. The worker is kept safe from contacting the blades by a guard.

At a print shop, a format worker is setting the text for printing.
Today this is done with computer programs.

This worker is physically moving paper to the printing machine.

The final process is the folding machine to fold papers.

# Chapter Four

# Concrete and Cement Products

A part of the concrete process is brick making. This is extruding brick material to be sliced into bricks and and then placed into kilns for curing.

A concrete engineer is operating a large cement making machine.

A worker bends rebar to be used to reinforce the concrete.

In another process, workers are tying rebar together
to fabricate a segment of a bridge replacement.

Then, concrete is poured over the rebar to make the bridge segment.

This worker is cleaning up the concrete pipe
after the concrete has hardened and cured.

# Chapter Five

# Wood Working

The heavy equipment operator is transporting logs to the saw mill.

A worker is operating a log debarking machine. By the engineer's directions, the blades scrape the bark from the log.

Using saws and shapers, the logs are turned into boards.

For this process. conveyor belts and laser beams ensure a perfect cut.

A boat builder is providing finishing touches on his hand-built boat.

The logs are soaked with water before they can be
used for wood veneer cutting. Workers are transporting
a log to a machine which will cut the wood veneer.

The firewood is kiln-dried before packaging for stores to sell.

The packaged firewood is ready to go.

Here a worker is operating a Bolter saw, which is considered unsafe by OSHA (Occupational Safety and Health Administration).

Workers are cutting wood in a "square mill",
making squares to be later turned into dowels.

Further processing in the square mill.

Assembling roofing trusses. Roofing trusses are used
to provide the skeleton for making a finished roof.

Quality Control: Note the speed of the worker's hand while inspecting the product. She wasn't pleased that I was in her space, but allowed me to photograph her.

Sanding wood takes time and patience.
Three workers are putting finishing touches on these frames.

# Chapter Six

# Healthcare

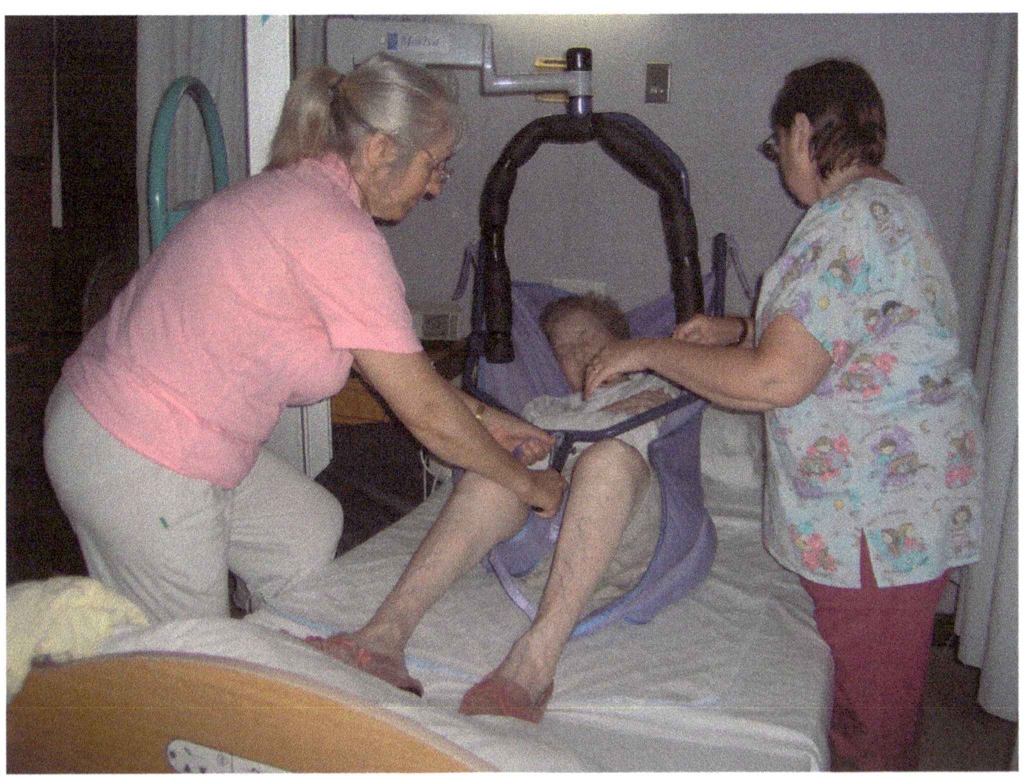

Health care workers assist compassionately to move a patient who cannot move herself. The woman was riddled with arthritis and all movement was painful.

Chefs are preparing food at a nursing home, a demanding task.

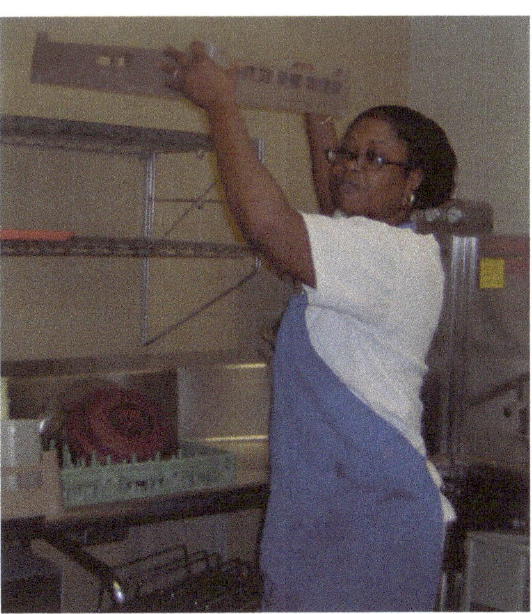

Cafeteria Workers have many physical chores, too.

[ABOVE] Commercial Laundry? Oh wait, this is a nursing home.

[AT LEFT] There is a lot of laundry in a healthcare facility that must be transported.

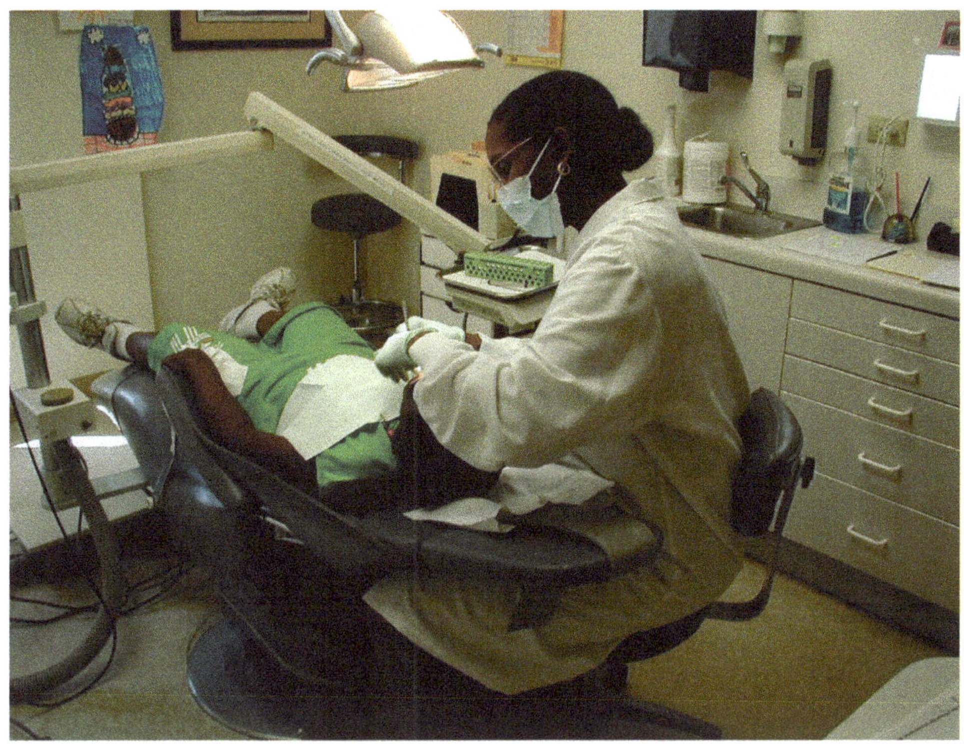

A dentist is practicing her profession.

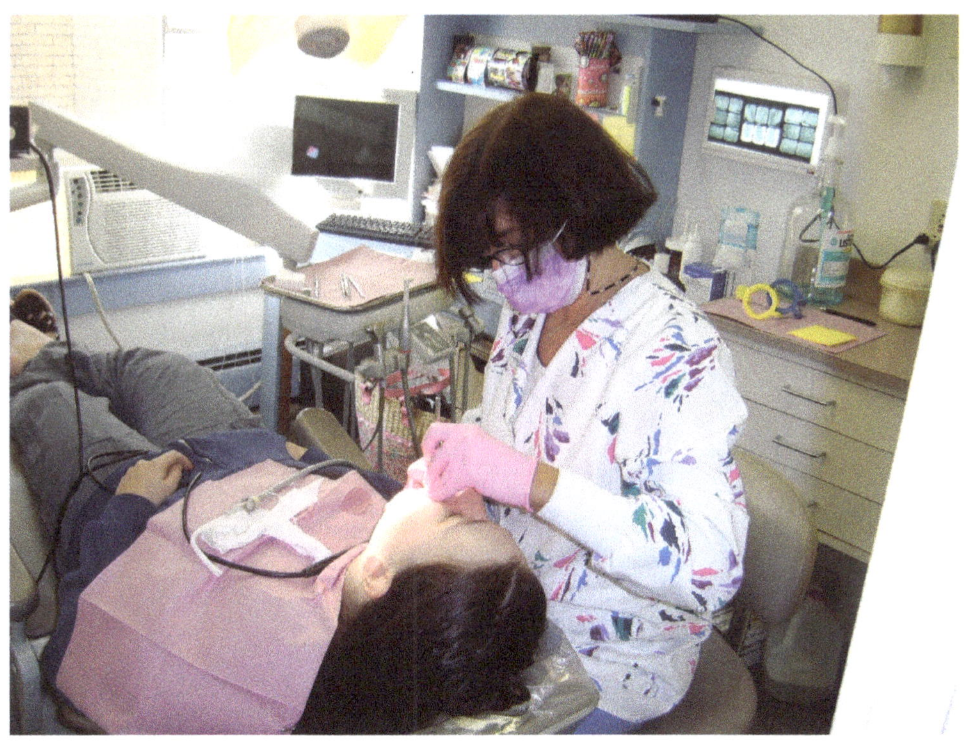

Here is a dental hygienist skillfully at work.

# Chapter Seven

# Food Processing

Milk production: Moving milk products from the cold room for shipment.

Checking the tank full of milk product to provide perfect program specifics.

Cheese Making is an involved process.
These workers are wringing out the cheese prior to packaging.

You need a manufacturing process to make popsicles.

Final packaging process for the popsicles.

# Chapter Eight

# Packaging and Transport of Materials

The worker is filling bags with sawdust which will be sold.
The process is monitored for dust inhalation.

Packaging a product, and securing that product in a solid cabinet, for shipment.

Warehousing: A fork truck driver is carefully removing product from shelves.

Warehousing: A different form of transporting product in a warehouse

[ABOVE] Loading inside a tractor trailer preparing for transport. The load must be secure.

[AT RIGHT] Loading the truck, to tightly pack the products, so they cannot rattle around during transport.

# Chapter Nine

# Service and Maintenance

A Chimney Sweep uses a long-handled tool
and brushes to clean out a chimney.

Taking apart a brick making machine using
the biggest wrench the author has ever seen.

Cleaning the "schmutz" out of a brick making machine. It's a dirty job.

A dust collector collects lots of dust and grime.
A high powered vacuum is needed to clean it out when it gets clogged.

In a Recycling Plant, a sorting line is where various materials are classified. Note the dust particles that appear as circles in the picture.

Boxes of waste paper are collected for recycling.

Saw blade expert: Saw blades of all shapes and sizes need to be repaired and sharpened. Reconditioning saw blades is an important skill.

Servicing printing
machines requires
cleaning, changing
ink and repair work.

A mechanic is fixing a faulty wire machine. The machine is off
and locked out by the mechanic to ensure the mechanic's safety.

[ABOVE]At the end of the work season, this large vessel must be cleaned out. Testing the air inside a ventilated tank is important to ensure that the air quality inside is safe for entry.

[AT LEFT] Old paint may contain lead. The worker is removing lead paint in a historic building using wet means to avoid the lead getting airborne.

# Chapter Ten

# The Ultimate Catastrophe

A first view of the devastation at the World Trade Center Complex on 9-12-2001.
How do workers keep safe during rescue, recovery and cleanup?

The perimeter of the devastation was being cleared to create a path to get onsite.

Firefighters are going through the rubble looking for any signs of life.
Over 22 agencies worked together making difficult decisions.

Firefighters are analyzing the devastation.

Most workers worked 12-hour shifts around the clock, seven days a week.

An overview of the 23-acre devastation of the
World Trade Center Complex, 2 months after the event.

Work surveyors checked the integrity of the wall hourly.
Wall separated the site from the river. A wall collapse would endanger all on site.

Workers clearing debris at the bottom of Manhattan.

High steel workers are taking a well-needed
break from cutting off pieces of collapsed steel.

# Acknowledgements

To Barbara Johnston, my new best friend, for lighting the fire to create this book.

To Sarah Johnston and Dennis Johnston for their enhancing and editing the photos in this book.

To Alenore Cusick, Ian Ross, Stephen Ross, Elizabeth Lepore, Diane Maguire, Christine Waters, Brandon Myers and Sharon Maby for editorial, Technical and moral support.